RAMADAN BEDTIME STORIES

STORIES

30 STORIES FOR 30 NIGHTS

TABLE OF CONTENTS :

TABLE OF CONTENTS :

RAMADAN MUBARAK, KIDS!

THIS IS A SPECIAL TIME OF THE YEAR FOR MUSLIMS ALL AROUND THE WORLD. DURING RAMADAN, WE FAST FROM DAWN TO DUSK, WHICH MEANS WE DON'T EAT OR DRINK ANYTHING DURING THE DAY. BUT IT'S NOT JUST ABOUT NOT EATING - IT'S ALSO A TIME TO FOCUS ON OUR FAITH AND TO DO GOOD DEEDS.

IN THIS BOOK, YOU'LL FIND 30 BEDTIME STORIES THAT WILL TEACH YOU ABOUT RAMADAN AND ITS IMPORTANCE. THESE STORIES ARE FUN, INSPIRING, AND BASED ON ISLAMIC TEACHINGS AND TRADITIONS. YOU'LL LEARN ABOUT THE FIRST REVELATION OF THE QURAN, THE IMPORTANCE OF PRAYER, THE STORIES OF THE PROPHETS, AND MANY OTHER THINGS.

WE HOPE THAT THESE STORIES WILL HELP
YOU UNDERSTAND MORE ABOUT RAMADAN
AND WHY IT'S SUCH A SPECIAL TIME FOR
MUSLIMS. WE ALSO HOPE THAT THEY WILL
INSPIRE YOU TO BE KIND, GENEROUS, AND
FAITHFUL, NOT JUST DURING RAMADAN BUT
ALL YEAR ROUND.

SO GET READY TO SNUGGLE UP AND LISTEN
TO SOME AMAZING BEDTIME STORIES THAT
WILL TAKE YOU ON A JOURNEY OF FAITH,
ADVENTURE, AND INSPIRATION. RAMADAN
KAREEM!

THE STORY OF THE FIRST REVELATION:

MORE THAN 1,400 YEARS AGO, A MAN NAMED MUHAMMAD (PEACE BE UPON HIM) LIVED IN MECCA, A CITY IN PRESENT-DAY SAUDI ARABIA. ONE DAY, WHEN HE WAS 40 YEARS OLD, HE WENT TO A CAVE CALLED HIRA TO PRAY AND MEDITATE.

AS HE SAT THERE, HE SUDDENLY HEARD A VOICE CALLING OUT TO HIM. THE VOICE SAID, "READ!" BUT MUHAMMAD (PEACE BE UPON HIM) WAS ILLITERATE AND DIDN'T KNOW HOW TO READ OR WRITE. SO HE REPLIED, "I CANNOT READ."

THE VOICE SPOKE AGAIN, SAYING, "READ! IN THE NAME OF YOUR LORD, WHO CREATED MAN FROM A CLOT OF BLOOD. READ, FOR YOUR LORD IS THE MOST GENEROUS, WHO TAUGHT BY THE PEN, TAUGHT MAN WHAT HE DID NOT KNOW."

THESE WORDS WERE THE FIRST VERSES OF THE QURAN, THE HOLY BOOK OF ISLAM. MUHAMMAD (PEACE BE UPON HIM) WAS AMAZED AND SCARED BY THE EXPERIENCE, BUT HE FELT COMPELLED TO SHARE THE MESSAGE HE HAD RECEIVED.

HE WENT TO HIS WIFE KHADIJAH AND TOLD
HER WHAT HAD HAPPENED. SHE BELIEVED IN
HIM AND HELPED HIM TO UNDERSTAND
THAT HE HAD BEEN CHOSEN BY ALLAH
(GOD) TO BE A PROPHET AND TO SPREAD
THE MESSAGE OF ISLAM.

AND SO BEGAN THE REVELATION OF THE
QURAN, WHICH CONTINUED OVER A PERIOD
OF 23 YEARS. MUHAMMAD (PEACE BE UPON
HIM) SHARED THE MESSAGE OF ISLAM WITH
HIS FAMILY, FRIENDS, AND COMMUNITY, AND
MANY PEOPLE BEGAN TO EMBRACE THE
FAITH.

THIS STORY TEACHES US ABOUT THE
IMPORTANCE OF LISTENING TO AND FOLLOWING
THE GUIDANCE OF ALLAH, AND THE ROLE OF
PROPHET MUHAMMAD (PEACE BE UPON HIM) AS
THE FINAL MESSENGER OF ALLAH.

IT ALSO HIGHLIGHTS THE IMPORTANCE OF
SUPPORT AND ENCOURAGEMENT FROM
LOVED ONES IN TIMES OF DOUBT AND
UNCERTAINTY.

THE STORY OF THE BLESSED MONTH

ONCE UPON A TIME, THERE WAS A BLESSED MONTH CALLED RAMADAN. RAMADAN WAS A SPECIAL MONTH THAT MUSLIMS ALL AROUND THE WORLD LOOKED FORWARD TO EVERY YEAR. IT WAS A MONTH OF FASTING, PRAYER, AND SPIRITUAL REFLECTION.

THE STORY OF RAMADAN BEGINS WITH THE SIGHTING OF THE NEW MOON. WHEN THE MOON IS SIGHTED, MUSLIMS KNOW THAT THE HOLY MONTH OF RAMADAN HAS BEGUN. MUSLIMS ALL AROUND THE WORLD WAKE UP EARLY IN THE MORNING TO EAT A MEAL CALLED SUHOOR BEFORE THE SUN RISES. THEY FAST DURING THE DAY, ABSTAINING FROM FOOD, DRINK, AND OTHER PHYSICAL NEEDS UNTIL THE SUN SETS.

DURING RAMADAN, MUSLIMS SPEND THEIR TIME READING THE QURAN, PERFORMING ACTS OF KINDNESS AND CHARITY, AND SPENDING TIME WITH THEIR FAMILIES. THEY BREAK THEIR FAST EVERY EVENING WITH A MEAL CALLED IFTAR. THEY ALSO GATHER AT THE MOSQUE FOR SPECIAL PRAYERS CALLED TARAWIH.

RAMADAN IS A MONTH OF PATIENCE AND SELF-DISCIPLINE. MUSLIMS USE THIS MONTH TO STRENGTHEN THEIR RELATIONSHIP WITH ALLAH AND TO IMPROVE THEIR CHARACTER. IT IS A TIME TO BE GRATEFUL FOR ALL THE BLESSINGS IN THEIR LIVES AND TO HELP THOSE WHO ARE LESS FORTUNATE.

AT THE END OF THE MONTH OF RAMADAN, MUSLIMS CELEBRATE THE FESTIVAL OF EID AL-FITR. IT IS A TIME OF JOY AND CELEBRATION, AND MUSLIMS ALL AROUND THE WORLD COME TOGETHER TO GIVE THANKS TO ALLAH FOR THE BLESSINGS THEY HAVE RECEIVED.

THE STORY OF RAMADAN TEACHES US MANY IMPORTANT LESSONS. IT REMINDS US TO BE GRATEFUL FOR ALL THE BLESSINGS IN OUR LIVES AND TO HELP THOSE WHO ARE LESS FORTUNATE. IT TEACHES US THE VALUE OF SELF-DISCIPLINE AND PATIENCE, AND IT STRENGTHENS OUR RELATIONSHIP WITH ALLAH. RAMADAN IS TRULY A BLESSED MONTH, AND MUSLIMS ALL AROUND THE WORLD CHERISH IT AND LOOK FORWARD TO IT EVERY YEAR. .

THE STORY OF THE FIVE PILLARS
OF ISLAM

ONCE UPON A TIME, THERE WAS A MAN NAMED MUHAMMAD WHO LIVED IN THE CITY OF MECCA. MUHAMMAD WAS A KIND AND HONEST MAN, AND HE WAS LOVED AND RESPECTED BY MANY PEOPLE IN HIS COMMUNITY.

ONE DAY, WHILE MUHAMMAD WAS MEDITATING IN A CAVE OUTSIDE THE CITY, HE RECEIVED A REVELATION FROM ALLAH. ALLAH REVEALED TO HIM THE TEACHINGS OF ISLAM, A NEW RELIGION THAT WOULD GUIDE PEOPLE TO THE PATH OF RIGHTEOUSNESS.

ONE OF THE MOST IMPORTANT TEACHINGS OF ISLAM ARE THE FIVE PILLARS, WHICH ARE THE FOUNDATION OF THE FAITH. THE FIVE PILLARS ARE
:

1. SHAHADA - THE DECLARATION OF FAITH IN ALLAH AND HIS PROPHET, MUHAMMAD.
2. SALAH - THE PERFORMANCE OF FIVE DAILY PRAYERS, FACING THE DIRECTION OF THE KAABA IN MECCA.
3. ZAKAT - THE GIVING OF CHARITY TO THOSE IN NEED.
4. SAWM - THE OBSERVANCE OF FASTING DURING THE HOLY MONTH OF RAMADAN.
5. HAJJ - THE PILGRIMAGE TO THE HOLY CITY OF MECCA AT LEAST ONCE IN A MUSLIM'S LIFETIME, IF ABLE.

MUHAMMAD TAUGHT HIS FOLLOWERS THAT THE
FIVE PILLARS WERE ESSENTIAL TO LEADING A GOOD
AND FULFILLING LIFE. HE ENCOURAGED THEM TO
PERFORM THESE ACTS OF WORSHIP WITH
SINCERITY AND DEVOTION, AND TO USE THEM AS A
MEANS OF GETTING CLOSER TO ALLAH.

DURING THE HOLY MONTH OF RAMADAN, MUSLIMS
ALL AROUND THE WORLD OBSERVE SAWM, THE
FOURTH PILLAR OF ISLAM. THEY FAST FROM DAWN
UNTIL SUNSET, ABSTAINING FROM FOOD, DRINK,
AND OTHER PHYSICAL NEEDS. THEY DO THIS TO
SHOW THEIR DEVOTION TO ALLAH AND TO REMIND
THEMSELVES OF THE BLESSINGS THEY HAVE
RECEIVED IN THEIR LIVES.

THE STORY OF THE FIVE PILLARS OF ISLAM
TEACHES US THE IMPORTANCE OF FAITH, PRAYER,
CHARITY, FASTING, AND PILGRIMAGE. IT REMINDS US
THAT THESE ACTS OF WORSHIP ARE A MEANS OF
GETTING CLOSER TO ALLAH, AND THAT THEY HELP
US LEAD A GOOD AND FULFILLING LIFE. MUSLIMS ALL
AROUND THE WORLD FOLLOW THESE PILLARS, AND
THEY ARE AN ESSENTIAL PART OF THEIR FAITH.

THE STORY OF THE NIGHT OF POWER

ONCE UPON A TIME, THERE WAS A SPECIAL NIGHT CALLED THE NIGHT OF POWER OR LAYLATUL QADR IN THE MONTH OF RAMADAN. THIS NIGHT WAS VERY IMPORTANT TO MUSLIMS ALL AROUND THE WORLD BECAUSE IT MARKED THE NIGHT WHEN THE FIRST VERSES OF THE QURAN WERE REVEALED TO PROPHET MUHAMMAD

THE NIGHT OF POWER IS BELIEVED TO BE A NIGHT OF GREAT BLESSINGS AND REWARDS. MUSLIMS BELIEVE THAT THE PRAYERS AND GOOD DEEDS PERFORMED ON THIS NIGHT ARE MULTIPLIED MANY TIMES OVER. IT IS SAID THAT THE NIGHT OF POWER IS BETTER THAN A THOUSAND MONTHS OF WORSHIP, AND THAT THOSE WHO SPEND THIS NIGHT IN WORSHIP AND DEVOTION WILL BE REWARDED WITH FORGIVENESS AND GUIDANCE FROM ALLAH.

PROPHET MUHAMMAD USED TO SPEND THE LAST TEN NIGHTS OF RAMADAN IN THE MOSQUE, DEVOTING HIMSELF TO PRAYER AND WORSHIP. ONE NIGHT, DURING THE LAST TEN NIGHTS OF RAMADAN, HE HAD A VISION IN WHICH HE WAS TOLD THAT THE NIGHT OF POWER WAS IN ONE OF THOSE NIGHTS. SO, HE URGED HIS FOLLOWERS TO SEEK OUT THIS SPECIAL NIGHT AND TO SPEND IT IN PRAYER AND DEVOTION.

MUSLIMS ALL AROUND THE WORLD SPEND THE NIGHT OF POWER IN PRAYER AND WORSHIP, RECITING THE QURAN, PERFORMING ACTS OF CHARITY, AND SEEKING FORGIVENESS FROM ALLAH. THEY STAY UP ALL NIGHT, SEEKING ALLAH'S GUIDANCE AND BLESSINGS, AND HOPING TO RECEIVE THE GREAT REWARDS THAT ARE PROMISED TO THEM .

THE NIGHT OF POWER IS A REMINDER TO MUSLIMS OF THE GREAT BLESSINGS AND REWARDS THAT ARE AVAILABLE TO THEM IF THEY WORSHIP ALLAH WITH SINCERITY AND DEVOTION. IT TEACHES THEM THE IMPORTANCE OF SEEKING FORGIVENESS AND GUIDANCE FROM ALLAH, AND IT REMINDS THEM OF THE GREAT GIFT OF THE QURAN, WHICH WAS REVEALED TO PROPHET MUHAMMAD ON THIS SPECIAL NIGHT.

SO, DURING THE HOLY MONTH OF RAMADAN, MUSLIMS ALL AROUND THE WORLD EAGERLY SEEK OUT THE NIGHT OF POWER, HOPING TO RECEIVE THE BLESSINGS AND REWARDS THAT ARE PROMISED TO THEM. THEY KNOW THAT THIS IS A SPECIAL NIGHT, A NIGHT OF GREAT MERCY AND FORGIVENESS, AND THEY DEVOTE THEMSELVES TO PRAYER AND WORSHIP, HOPING TO DRAW CLOSER TO ALLAH AND TO RECEIVE HIS GUIDANCE AND BLESSINGS.

THE STORY OF THE BATTLE OF BADR

ONCE UPON A TIME, THERE WAS A FAMOUS
BATTLE CALLED THE BATTLE OF BADR THAT
TOOK PLACE DURING THE TIME OF PROPHET
MUHAMMAD. THIS BATTLE WAS FOUGHT
BETWEEN THE MUSLIMS OF MEDINA AND THE
POLYTHEISTS OF MECCA, WHO HAD BEEN
PERSECUTING THE MUSLIMS FOR YEARS.

THE BATTLE OF BADR TOOK PLACE IN THE
MONTH OF RAMADAN, IN THE SECOND YEAR
OF THE HIJRA (MIGRATION OF THE MUSLIMS
FROM MECCA TO MEDINA). THE MUSLIMS
WERE OUTNUMBERED AND POORLY
EQUIPPED, WHILE THE MECCANS HAD A
WELL-EQUIPPED ARMY AND WERE
CONFIDENT OF VICTORY.

HOWEVER, THE MUSLIMS WERE DETERMINED
TO DEFEND THEIR FAITH AND THEIR
COMMUNITY, AND THEY PUT THEIR TRUST IN
ALLAH. PROPHET MUHAMMAD LED THE
MUSLIMS INTO BATTLE, AND THEY FOUGHT
BRAVELY AGAINST THE MECCANS.

DESPITE BEING OUTNUMBERED, THE MUSLIMS WON THE BATTLE, AND THIS WAS SEEN AS A GREAT VICTORY FOR THE MUSLIMS. THIS VICTORY SHOWED THE STRENGTH AND DETERMINATION OF THE MUSLIMS, AND IT INSPIRED THEM TO CONTINUE FIGHTING FOR THEIR FAITH AND THEIR COMMUNITY.

THE BATTLE OF BADR IS A REMINDER TO MUSLIMS OF THE IMPORTANCE OF STANDING UP FOR THEIR FAITH AND THEIR COMMUNITY, EVEN IN THE FACE OF GREAT CHALLENGES AND ADVERSITY. IT TEACHES THEM THE IMPORTANCE OF RELYING ON ALLAH AND PUTTING THEIR TRUST IN HIM, AND IT REMINDS THEM OF THE BRAVERY AND SACRIFICE OF THEIR ANCESTORS.

DURING THE HOLY MONTH OF RAMADAN, MUSLIMS ALL AROUND THE WORLD REMEMBER THE BATTLE OF BADR AND THE GREAT VICTORY THAT WAS ACHIEVED THROUGH THE POWER OF FAITH AND DETERMINATION. THEY ARE INSPIRED BY THE BRAVERY AND SACRIFICE OF THEIR ANCESTORS, AND THEY STRIVE TO FOLLOW IN THEIR FOOTSTEPS BY STANDING UP FOR THEIR FAITH AND THEIR COMMUNITY, AND BY RELYING ON ALLAH FOR GUIDANCE AND STRENGTH.

THE STORY OF IFTAR

ONCE UPON A TIME, IN A SMALL VILLAGE, LIVED A YOUNG BOY NAMED OMAR. HE WAS EAGERLY WAITING FOR THE HOLY MONTH OF RAMADAN TO BEGIN. RAMADAN IS A MONTH OF FASTING, PRAYER, AND SPIRITUAL REFLECTION FOR MUSLIMS ALL AROUND THE WORLD. OMAR LOVED THE SENSE OF COMMUNITY AND TOGETHERNESS THAT CAME WITH THIS SPECIAL MONTH.

AS THE MONTH OF RAMADAN STARTED, OMAR'S FAMILY BEGAN THEIR FAST EVERY DAY BEFORE SUNRISE AND WOULD BREAK THEIR FAST AT SUNSET. OMAR'S MOTHER WOULD PREPARE A DELICIOUS MEAL EVERY EVENING, WHICH THEY WOULD ALL EAGERLY WAIT FOR. OMAR WOULD HELP HIS MOTHER PREPARE FOR IFTAR, THE MEAL THAT IS EATEN AFTER SUNSET TO BREAK THE FAST.

ONE EVENING, AS THEY WERE PREPARING FOR IFTAR, THEY HEARD A KNOCK ON THEIR DOOR. IT WAS A POOR AND HUNGRY MAN WHO HAD NOTHING TO EAT FOR IFTAR. OMAR'S MOTHER WELCOMED HIM IN AND INVITED HIM TO JOIN THEM FOR THEIR MEAL. THEY ALL SAT DOWN TOGETHER, AND OMAR'S MOTHER SERVED THEM DATES AND WATER TO BREAK THEIR FAST.

14

THE POOR MAN WAS OVERWHELMED WITH
GRATITUDE AND THANKED OMAR'S FAMILY
FOR THEIR KINDNESS. OMAR AND HIS FAMILY
FELT HAPPY AND CONTENT FOR SHARING
THEIR MEAL WITH SOMEONE IN NEED.

FROM THAT DAY ONWARDS, OMAR AND HIS FAMILY
MADE IT A TRADITION TO INVITE SOMEONE LESS
FORTUNATE TO SHARE THEIR IFTAR MEAL EVERY
DAY DURING THE MONTH OF RAMADAN. THEY
WOULD DONATE FOOD AND MONEY TO THE NEEDY
AND MAKE SURE NO ONE WENT HUNGRY DURING
THIS BLESSED MONTH.

AS THE MONTH OF RAMADAN CAME TO AN
END, OMAR AND HIS FAMILY FELT GRATEFUL
FOR THE BLESSINGS THEY HAD RECEIVED
AND THE OPPORTUNITY TO SHARE THEM
WITH OTHERS. THEY HAD LEARNED THAT
RAMADAN IS NOT JUST ABOUT FASTING AND
PRAYER BUT ALSO ABOUT KINDNESS,
COMPASSION, AND GIVING BACK TO THE
COMMUNITY.

AND THAT, MY DEAR LITTLE ONES, IS THE
STORY OF HOW OMAR AND HIS FAMILY
MADE IFTAR A SPECIAL TIME FOR SHARING
AND GIVING DURING THE HOLY MONTH OF
RAMADAN.

THE STORY OF EID AL-FITR

ONCE UPON A TIME, IN THE HOLY MONTH OF RAMADAN, MUSLIMS ALL AROUND THE WORLD FASTED DURING THE DAY AND SPENT THEIR TIME IN PRAYER AND REFLECTION. THEY WORKED HARD TO IMPROVE THEIR FAITH AND BE KIND TO OTHERS. AND WHEN THE MONTH OF RAMADAN CAME TO AN END, IT WAS TIME TO CELEBRATE EID AL-FITR

EID AL-FITR IS A SPECIAL FESTIVAL THAT MARKS THE END OF THE MONTH OF RAMADAN. MUSLIMS CELEBRATE THIS DAY WITH GREAT JOY AND HAPPINESS. THEY WAKE UP EARLY IN THE MORNING, WEAR NEW CLOTHES, AND HEAD OUT TO THE MOSQUE FOR THE EID PRAYER. PEOPLE GREET EACH OTHER WITH THE WORDS "EID MUBARAK," WHICH MEANS "BLESSED EID."

AFTER THE EID PRAYER, FAMILIES GATHER TOGETHER TO ENJOY A DELICIOUS FEAST. THEY SHARE FOOD AND GIFTS WITH EACH OTHER AND EXCHANGE HUGS AND WELL-WISHES. CHILDREN RECEIVE MONEY AND GIFTS FROM THEIR ELDERS, WHICH THEY EAGERLY LOOK FORWARD TO.

16

BUT EID AL-FITR IS NOT JUST ABOUT EATING AND GIFTS. IT IS ALSO A TIME FOR FORGIVENESS AND MAKING AMENDS. MUSLIMS SEEK FORGIVENESS FROM GOD AND FROM EACH OTHER. THEY VISIT THEIR RELATIVES AND FRIENDS TO STRENGTHEN THEIR RELATIONSHIPS AND SPREAD JOY AND HAPPINESS.

ONE YEAR, A MAN NAMED ALI HAD A DISAGREEMENT WITH HIS FRIEND, AHMED. THEY HAD ARGUED OVER SOMETHING TRIVIAL, AND THEIR FRIENDSHIP HAD SUFFERED. BUT ON THE DAY OF EID AL-FITR, ALI DECIDED TO REACH OUT TO AHMED AND APOLOGIZE. HE REALIZED THAT THEIR FRIENDSHIP WAS MORE IMPORTANT THAN THEIR DISAGREEMENT.

AHMED ACCEPTED ALI'S APOLOGY, AND THEY HUGGED EACH OTHER TIGHTLY. THEY SPENT THE DAY TOGETHER, ENJOYING THE FESTIVITIES AND MAKING NEW MEMORIES.

AND THAT, MY DEAR LITTLE ONES, IS THE STORY OF EID AL-FITR. IT IS A DAY OF HAPPINESS, FORGIVENESS, AND TOGETHERNESS. IT REMINDS US TO BE KIND TO OTHERS, SEEK FORGIVENESS, AND CHERISH OUR RELATIONSHIPS.

THE STORY OF SADAQAH

ONCE UPON A TIME, IN A SMALL VILLAGE, LIVED A YOUNG GIRL NAMED AISHA. AISHA WAS A KIND AND GENEROUS GIRL WHO LOVED TO HELP THOSE IN NEED. SHE WOULD OFTEN GIVE HER POCKET MONEY TO THE POOR AND NEEDY PEOPLE IN HER VILLAGE.

ONE DAY, DURING THE HOLY MONTH OF RAMADAN, AISHA SAW AN OLD MAN SITTING BY THE SIDE OF THE ROAD. HE LOOKED TIRED AND HUNGRY. AISHA WENT UP TO HIM AND ASKED HIM WHAT WAS WRONG. THE OLD MAN TOLD HER THAT HE HAD NOT EATEN ANYTHING ALL DAY AND WAS FEELING WEAK.

AISHA FELT SORRY FOR THE OLD MAN AND KNEW THAT SHE HAD TO DO SOMETHING TO HELP HIM. SHE REMEMBERED THE IMPORTANCE OF SADAQAH, WHICH MEANS GIVING CHARITY, ESPECIALLY DURING RAMADAN. SHE TOOK THE OLD MAN TO HER HOME AND GAVE HIM SOME FOOD AND WATER. SHE ALSO GAVE HIM SOME MONEY SO THAT HE COULD BUY FOOD FOR HIMSELF.

THE OLD MAN WAS VERY GRATEFUL TO AISHA
AND BLESSED HER. HE TOLD HER THAT HER
KINDNESS WOULD NOT GO UNNOTICED AND
THAT SHE WOULD BE REWARDED FOR HER
GOOD DEEDS

FROM THAT DAY ONWARDS, AISHA MADE IT A
HABIT TO GIVE SADAQAH EVERY DAY DURING
RAMADAN. SHE WOULD GIVE HER POCKET
MONEY TO THE POOR AND NEEDY PEOPLE IN
HER VILLAGE. SHE ALSO ENCOURAGED HER
FRIENDS AND FAMILY TO GIVE SADAQAH AND
HELP THOSE IN NEED.

AS THE MONTH OF RAMADAN CAME TO AN END,
AISHA FELT HAPPY AND CONTENT FOR HELPING
OTHERS. SHE HAD LEARNED THAT SADAQAH IS
NOT JUST ABOUT GIVING MONEY, BUT IT IS ALSO
ABOUT GIVING YOUR TIME, YOUR LOVE, AND
YOUR KINDNESS TO OTHERS.

AND THAT, MY DEAR LITTLE ONES, IS THE STORY
OF HOW AISHA LEARNED THE IMPORTANCE OF
SADAQAH DURING RAMADAN. IT TEACHES US
THAT GIVING CHARITY IS NOT JUST A RELIGIOUS
OBLIGATION, BUT IT IS ALSO A WAY TO HELP
THOSE IN NEED AND SPREAD KINDNESS IN THE
WORLD.

THE STORY OF THE PROPHET IBRAHIM

ONCE UPON A TIME, THERE WAS A PROPHET NAMED IBRAHIM. HE WAS A GREAT AND WISE MAN WHO LOVED ALLAH VERY MUCH. HE LIVED IN A LAND WHERE MOST OF THE PEOPLE WORSHIPPED IDOLS, BUT IBRAHIM BELIEVED IN THE ONE TRUE GOD.

ONE NIGHT, IBRAHIM HAD A DREAM WHERE HE SAW HIMSELF SACRIFICING HIS SON ISMAIL. HE KNEW THAT THIS WAS A COMMAND FROM ALLAH AND HE WOKE UP DETERMINED TO FULFILL IT. HE WENT TO HIS SON ISMAIL AND TOLD HIM ABOUT THE DREAM. ISMAIL WAS A GOOD AND OBEDIENT SON AND HE AGREED TO THE SACRIFICE

THE TWO OF THEM WENT TO A REMOTE PLACE WHERE THERE WAS NOBODY AROUND. IBRAHIM RAISED HIS KNIFE TO SACRIFICE HIS SON, BUT JUST AS HE WAS ABOUT TO DO IT, ALLAH SENT AN ANGEL TO STOP HIM. THE ANGEL TOLD IBRAHIM THAT HE HAD PASSED THE TEST AND THAT HE DID NOT HAVE TO SACRIFICE HIS SON. INSTEAD, ALLAH PROVIDED A RAM FOR THE SACRIFICE.

IBRAHIM AND ISMAIL WERE BOTH GRATEFUL TO ALLAH FOR HIS MERCY AND THEY CONTINUED TO WORSHIP HIM. AS THE YEARS WENT BY, IBRAHIM BECAME KNOWN AS THE FATHER OF THE PROPHETS, AS HE HAD MANY CHILDREN WHO ALSO BECAME PROPHETS.

THE STORY OF PROPHET IBRAHIM TEACHES US ABOUT THE IMPORTANCE OF OBEYING ALLAH AND HAVING FAITH IN HIM. IT ALSO REMINDS US THAT ALLAH IS MERCIFUL AND JUST, AND THAT HE WILL ALWAYS PROVIDE FOR THOSE WHO TRUST IN HIM.

AND WITH THAT, THE LITTLE ONES DRIFTED OFF TO SLEEP, DREAMING OF THE WISDOM AND KINDNESS OF ALLAH, AND THE BRAVERY AND FAITH OF PROPHET IBRAHIM.

THE STORY OF ZAKAT

ONCE UPON A TIME, THERE WAS A YOUNG BOY
NAMED ALI. ALI LIVED IN A SMALL VILLAGE WITH HIS
PARENTS AND SIBLINGS. ONE DAY, DURING THE
HOLY MONTH OF RAMADAN, ALI'S FATHER SAT HIM
DOWN AND EXPLAINED TO HIM THE IMPORTANCE
OF ZAKAT.

"ZAKAT IS A WAY OF GIVING TO THOSE WHO ARE
LESS FORTUNATE," ALI'S FATHER SAID. "IT IS ONE
OF THE PILLARS OF ISLAM AND IT IS OUR DUTY AS
MUSLIMS TO GIVE ZAKAT."

ALI LISTENED CAREFULLY TO HIS FATHER'S
WORDS AND WAS INSPIRED TO DO HIS PART TO
HELP OTHERS. HE DECIDED TO START A CHARITY
DRIVE IN HIS VILLAGE TO COLLECT MONEY FOR
THOSE IN NEED.

ALI WENT DOOR TO DOOR IN HIS VILLAGE,
EXPLAINING THE IMPORTANCE OF ZAKAT AND
ASKING FOR DONATIONS. MANY PEOPLE WERE
TOUCHED BY HIS DEDICATION AND GENEROSITY
AND THEY GAVE WHAT THEY COULD.

AT THE END OF THE CHARITY DRIVE, ALI HAD COLLECTED A SIGNIFICANT AMOUNT OF MONEY. HE WAS OVERJOYED THAT HE HAD BEEN ABLE TO MAKE A DIFFERENCE IN THE LIVES OF OTHERS.

ALI'S FATHER WAS VERY PROUD OF HIM AND EXPLAINED THAT ZAKAT IS NOT ONLY ABOUT GIVING MONEY, BUT ALSO ABOUT GIVING OUR TIME AND SKILLS TO HELP OTHERS. HE ENCOURAGED ALI TO CONTINUE TO GIVE BACK TO HIS COMMUNITY AND TO ALWAYS REMEMBER THE IMPORTANCE OF ZAKAT.

FROM THAT DAY ON, ALI MADE A PROMISE TO HIMSELF TO CONTINUE TO GIVE ZAKAT AND TO HELP THOSE IN NEED. HE LEARNED THAT EVEN SMALL ACTS OF KINDNESS CAN MAKE A BIG DIFFERENCE IN THE WORLD.

AND WITH THAT, ALI WENT TO SLEEP WITH A SMILE ON HIS FACE, FEELING GRATEFUL FOR THE BLESSINGS IN HIS LIFE AND EAGER TO CONTINUE GIVING TO THOSE IN NEED.

.THE STORY OF THE PROPHET MUSA

ONCE UPON A TIME, THERE WAS A PROPHET NAMED MUSA (MOSES). HE WAS BORN IN EGYPT DURING A TIME WHEN THE PHARAOH WAS OPPRESSING THE ISRAELITES. WHEN MUSA WAS BORN, HIS MOTHER PUT HIM IN A BASKET AND SET HIM ADRIFT ON THE RIVER. HE WAS FOUND BY THE PHARAOH'S WIFE AND RAISED AS HER OWN SON.

AS MUSA GREW OLDER, HE LEARNED ABOUT HIS TRUE IDENTITY AND BECAME TROUBLED BY THE WAY THE PHARAOH TREATED THE ISRAELITES. ONE DAY, HE SAW AN EGYPTIAN SOLDIER MISTREATING AN ISRAELITE AND HE INTERVENED, KILLING THE SOLDIER IN THE PROCESS. MUSA FLED EGYPT AND WENT TO THE DESERT WHERE HE LIVED AS A SHEPHERD FOR MANY YEARS.

ONE DAY, WHILE MUSA WAS TENDING HIS SHEEP, HE SAW A BURNING BUSH. THE BUSH WAS ON FIRE, BUT IT WAS NOT BEING CONSUMED BY THE FLAMES. MUSA APPROACHED THE BUSH AND HEARD THE VOICE OF ALLAH SPEAKING TO HIM.

"ALLAH TOLD MUSA THAT HE WAS CHOSEN TO BE A PROPHET AND TO LEAD THE ISRAELITES OUT OF SLAVERY IN EGYPT," SAID ALI'S FATHER, WHO WAS TELLING HIM THE STORY. "MUSA WAS HESITANT AT FIRST, BUT HE EVENTUALLY AGREED TO DO AS ALLAH COMMANDED."

MUSA WENT BACK TO EGYPT AND, WITH THE HELP OF HIS BROTHER HARUN (AARON), HE CONFRONTED THE PHARAOH AND DEMANDED THAT HE LET THE ISRAELITES GO. THE PHARAOH REFUSED AND ALLAH SENT MANY PLAGUES TO EGYPT TO CONVINCE THE PHARAOH TO FREE THE ISRAELITES. EVENTUALLY, THE PHARAOH RELENTED AND THE ISRAELITES WERE ABLE TO LEAVE EGYPT.

MUSA LED THE ISRAELITES THROUGH THE DESERT FOR MANY YEARS, AND DURING THAT TIME, HE RECEIVED THE TEN COMMANDMENTS FROM ALLAH ON MOUNT SINAI. HE TAUGHT THE ISRAELITES ABOUT THE LAWS AND COMMANDMENTS OF ALLAH AND LED THEM TO THE PROMISED LAND.

THE STORY OF PROPHET MUSA TEACHES US ABOUT THE IMPORTANCE OF STANDING UP FOR WHAT IS RIGHT AND HELPING THOSE WHO ARE OPPRESSED. IT ALSO REMINDS US THAT ALLAH IS ALWAYS WATCHING OVER US AND THAT HE WILL GUIDE US ON THE RIGHT PATH IF WE TRUST IN HIM.

AND WITH THAT, ALI WENT TO SLEEP, FEELING INSPIRED BY THE BRAVERY AND FAITH OF PROPHET MUSA AND EAGER TO FOLLOW IN HIS FOOTSTEPS.

THE STORY OF THE PROPHET YUSUF

ONCE UPON A TIME, THERE WAS A PROPHET NAMED YUSUF (JOSEPH). HE WAS THE SON OF PROPHET YAQUB (JACOB) AND HE HAD ELEVEN BROTHERS. YUSUF WAS A SPECIAL CHILD, AS HIS FATHER LOVED HIM MORE THAN HIS OTHER CHILDREN. THIS CAUSED JEALOUSY AND RESENTMENT AMONG YUSUF'S BROTHERS.

ONE DAY, YUSUF'S BROTHERS DECIDED TO SELL HIM INTO SLAVERY AND TOLD THEIR FATHER THAT HE HAD BEEN KILLED BY A WILD ANIMAL. YUSUF WAS TAKEN TO EGYPT AND SOLD TO A WEALTHY MAN NAMED POTIPHAR.

IN EGYPT, YUSUF FACED MANY CHALLENGES, BUT HE REMAINED FAITHFUL TO ALLAH AND CONTINUED TO PRAY AND TRUST IN HIM. YUSUF BECAME A TRUSTED SERVANT OF POTIPHAR AND WAS PUT IN CHARGE OF HIS HOUSEHOLD.

HOWEVER, YUSUF'S FAITH WAS TESTED ONCE AGAIN WHEN POTIPHAR'S WIFE TRIED TO SEDUCE HIM. YUSUF REFUSED HER ADVANCES AND SHE ACCUSED HIM OF TRYING TO SEDUCE HER. YUSUF WAS THROWN INTO PRISON, BUT HE CONTINUED TO PRAY AND TRUST IN ALLAH.

IN PRISON, YUSUF MET TWO MEN WHO HAD ALSO BEEN IMPRISONED. THEY BOTH HAD DREAMS, AND YUSUF INTERPRETED THEIR DREAMS FOR THEM. ONE MAN'S DREAM WAS A GOOD OMEN, AND YUSUF TOLD HIM THAT HE WOULD SOON BE RELEASED FROM PRISON. THE OTHER MAN'S DREAM WAS A BAD OMEN, AND YUSUF TOLD HIM THAT HE WOULD BE EXECUTED.

YUSUF'S INTERPRETATIONS OF THE DREAMS CAME TRUE, AND THE MAN WHO HAD BEEN RELEASED FROM PRISON REMEMBERED YUSUF'S KINDNESS AND TOLD THE PHARAOH ABOUT HIM. THE PHARAOH HAD A DREAM THAT HE COULD NOT UNDERSTAND, AND THE MAN

RECOMMENDED YUSUF TO INTERPRET IT. YUSUF INTERPRETED THE PHARAOH'S DREAM, AND HE WAS MADE THE GOVERNOR OF EGYPT. YUSUF'S WISDOM AND FAIRNESS HELPED EGYPT PROSPER DURING A TIME OF FAMINE, AND HIS FAMILY CAME TO EGYPT TO SEEK HIS HELP.

WHEN YUSUF'S BROTHERS CAME TO HIM, THEY DID NOT RECOGNIZE HIM, BUT YUSUF FORGAVE THEM AND REUNITED WITH HIS FAMILY. YUSUF'S STORY TEACHES US ABOUT THE IMPORTANCE OF FORGIVENESS AND TRUSTING IN ALLAH, EVEN DURING DIFFICULT TIMES.

AND WITH THAT, THE LITTLE ONE DRIFTED OFF TO SLEEP, DREAMING OF THE BRAVERY AND FAITH OF PROPHET YUSUF AND THE KINDNESS AND MERCY OF ALLAH.

THE STORY OF THE PROPHET DAWUD

ONCE UPON A TIME, THERE WAS A PROPHET
NAMED DAWUD (DAVID). HE WAS BORN IN
BETHLEHEM AND WAS THE YOUNGEST OF
HIS FAMILY. DAWUD WAS A SHEPHERD AND
SPENT MOST OF HIS TIME OUTDOORS
TAKING CARE OF HIS SHEEP.

ONE DAY, WHILE DAWUD WAS TENDING HIS
SHEEP, A LION ATTACKED ONE OF THEM.
DAWUD WAS ABLE TO FIGHT OFF THE LION
AND SAVE HIS SHEEP. THIS ACT OF BRAVERY
CAUGHT THE ATTENTION OF THE PEOPLE OF
HIS VILLAGE, AND SOON DAWUD BECAME
KNOWN FOR HIS STRENGTH AND COURAGE

AS DAWUD GREW OLDER, ALLAH CHOSE HIM
TO BE A PROPHET AND A LEADER OF HIS
PEOPLE. HE WAS KNOWN FOR HIS WISDOM,
AND HE WAS BLESSED WITH MANY GIFTS,
INCLUDING THE ABILITY TO PLAY THE HARP
AND SING BEAUTIFUL SONGS.

ONE OF THE MOST FAMOUS STORIES ABOUT
DAWUD IS HIS BATTLE WITH THE GIANT
WARRIOR GOLIATH. GOLIATH WAS A GIANT
WHO TERRORIZED THE PEOPLE OF HIS
VILLAGE, AND NO ONE WAS BRAVE ENOUGH
TO CHALLENGE HIM IN BATTLE. BUT DAWUD,
WITH HIS FAITH IN ALLAH AND HIS COURAGE,
VOLUNTEERED TO FIGHT GOLIATH.

DAWUD PICKED UP FIVE STONES FROM A
NEARBY STREAM AND USED HIS
SLINGSHOT TO HURL ONE OF THE
STONES AT GOLIATH. THE STONE HIT
GOLIATH IN THE FOREHEAD, AND HE FELL
TO THE GROUND. DAWUD THEN USED
GOLIATH'S OWN SWORD TO BEHEAD HIM,
AND THE PEOPLE WERE AMAZED AT
DAWUD'S BRAVERY

AFTER THIS BATTLE, DAWUD BECAME THE
KING OF HIS PEOPLE AND RULED WITH
JUSTICE AND FAIRNESS. HE WAS ALSO
KNOWN FOR HIS DEVOTION TO ALLAH
AND HIS BEAUTIFUL SONGS OF PRAISE.
DAWUD'S STORY TEACHES US ABOUT THE
IMPORTANCE OF COURAGE, WISDOM, AND
FAITH IN ALLAH, AND HOW THESE
QUALITIES CAN HELP US OVERCOME EVEN
THE GREATEST OF CHALLENGES.

AND WITH THAT, THE LITTLE ONE DRIFTED
OFF TO SLEEP, DREAMING OF THE
BRAVERY AND FAITH OF PROPHET DAWUD
AND THE WISDOM AND GUIDANCE OF
ALLAH.

THE STORY OF THE PROPHET SULAIMAN

ONCE UPON A TIME, THERE WAS A PROPHET NAMED SULAIMAN (SOLOMON). HE WAS THE SON OF PROPHET DAWUD (DAVID) AND WAS KNOWN FOR HIS WISDOM, WEALTH, AND ABILITY TO COMMUNICATE WITH ANIMALS AND JINN (SUPERNATURAL CREATURES).

SULAIMAN WAS CHOSEN BY ALLAH TO BE A PROPHET AND A LEADER OF HIS PEOPLE. HE WAS BLESSED WITH MANY GIFTS, INCLUDING THE ABILITY TO UNDERSTAND THE LANGUAGE OF ANIMALS AND JINN, AND THE POWER TO CONTROL THE WIND AND THE SEAS.

ONE DAY, SULAIMAN HEARD THE STORY OF THE QUEEN OF SHEBA, WHO WAS SAID TO BE THE RULER OF A WEALTHY AND POWERFUL KINGDOM. HE DECIDED TO SEND A MESSAGE TO HER, INVITING HER TO COME AND VISIT HIM IN HIS KINGDOM.

WHEN THE QUEEN OF SHEBA ARRIVED, SHE WAS IMPRESSED BY SULAIMAN'S WEALTH AND WISDOM. THEY HAD A LONG CONVERSATION, AND SULAIMAN SHOWED HER MANY OF HIS MARVELS, INCLUDING HIS PALACE AND HIS THRONE, WHICH WAS MADE OF GOLD AND ENCRUSTED WITH JEWELS.

DURING THEIR CONVERSATION, THE QUEEN OF SHEBA REALIZED THAT SULAIMAN WAS A TRUE PROPHET OF ALLAH, AND SHE BECAME A BELIEVER. SHE PRAISED ALLAH FOR THE BLESSINGS HE HAD GIVEN SULAIMAN AND HIS PEOPLE.

ANOTHER FAMOUS STORY ABOUT SULAIMAN IS HIS ABILITY TO UNDERSTAND THE LANGUAGE OF BIRDS. ONE DAY, SULAIMAN HEARD A BIRD CRYING OUT IN DISTRESS, AND HE UNDERSTOOD THAT IT WAS CALLING FOR HELP. HE DISCOVERED THAT A GROUP OF ANTS WERE IN DANGER OF BEING CRUSHED BY AN APPROACHING ARMY.

SULAIMAN COMMANDED THE BIRDS TO CARRY THE ANTS TO SAFETY, AND THEY OBEYED HIM. THIS ACT OF COMPASSION AND UNDERSTANDING EARNED SULAIMAN THE RESPECT OF THE ANIMALS AND THE PEOPLE.

SULAIMAN'S STORY TEACHES US ABOUT THE IMPORTANCE OF WISDOM, COMPASSION, AND UNDERSTANDING, AND HOW THESE QUALITIES CAN HELP US LEAD A SUCCESSFUL AND FULFILLING LIFE. AND WITH THAT, THE LITTLE ONE DRIFTED OFF TO SLEEP, DREAMING OF THE WISDOM AND POWER OF PROPHET SULAIMAN AND THE BLESSINGS AND GUIDANCE OF ALLAH.

THE STORY OF LAYLATUL QADR

ONCE UPON A TIME, DURING THE HOLY MONTH
OF RAMADAN, THE PROPHET MUHAMMAD (PEACE
BE UPON HIM) RECEIVED A REVELATION FROM
ALLAH ABOUT A SPECIAL NIGHT CALLED LAYLATUL
QADR (THE NIGHT OF POWER).

LAYLATUL QADR IS A NIGHT THAT IS BETTER THAN
A THOUSAND MONTHS, AND IT IS BELIEVED TO BE
THE NIGHT WHEN THE FIRST VERSES OF THE
QURAN WERE REVEALED TO THE PROPHET
MUHAMMAD (PEACE BE UPON HIM).

THE PROPHET MUHAMMAD (PEACE BE UPON HIM)
TOLD HIS FOLLOWERS ABOUT THE IMPORTANCE
OF LAYLATUL QADR AND ENCOURAGED THEM TO
SEEK IT OUT DURING THE LAST TEN DAYS OF
RAMADAN. HE SAID THAT WHOEVER PRAYS ON
THIS NIGHT WITH FAITH AND SINCERITY WILL HAVE
THEIR SINS FORGIVEN AND WILL BE REWARDED
WITH GREAT BLESSINGS FROM ALLAH.

THE PROPHET MUHAMMAD (PEACE BE UPON HIM)
ALSO TAUGHT HIS FOLLOWERS TO MAKE DUA
(SUPPLICATION) ON THIS NIGHT AND TO ASK FOR
FORGIVENESS AND GUIDANCE FROM ALLAH. HE
SAID THAT ALLAH IS MOST MERCIFUL ON THIS
NIGHT AND THAT WHOEVER ASKS FOR
FORGIVENESS WILL BE FORGIVEN.

TO HELP HIS FOLLOWERS FIND LAYLATUL
QADR, THE PROPHET MUHAMMAD (PEACE BE
UPON HIM) SUGGESTED THAT THEY SHOULD
LOOK FOR IT DURING THE ODD-NUMBERED
NIGHTS OF THE LAST TEN DAYS OF RAMADAN.
HE ALSO SAID THAT THE SIGNS OF LAYLATUL
QADR INCLUDE A FEELING OF PEACE AND
TRANQUILITY, THE SKY BEING FREE OF
CLOUDS, AND A BRIGHT LIGHT SHINING FROM
THE EAST.

THE STORY OF LAYLATUL QADR TEACHES US
ABOUT THE IMPORTANCE OF SEEKING ALLAH'S
FORGIVENESS AND GUIDANCE, AND THE
BLESSINGS THAT CAN BE OBTAINED THROUGH
FAITH AND SINCERITY. IT ALSO REMINDS US OF
THE SPECIAL NATURE OF RAMADAN AND THE
OPPORTUNITY IT PROVIDES TO DEEPEN OUR
CONNECTION WITH ALLAH AND SEEK HIS
BLESSINGS.

AND WITH THAT, THE LITTLE ONE DRIFTED OFF
TO SLEEP, DREAMING OF THE BLESSINGS OF
LAYLATUL QADR AND THE GUIDANCE AND
MERCY OF ALLAH.

THE STORY OF THE PROPHET ISA

ONCE UPON A TIME, THERE WAS A PROPHET NAMED ISA (JESUS) WHO WAS BORN TO THE VIRGIN MARYAM (MARY) IN PALESTINE. PROPHET ISA WAS CHOSEN BY ALLAH TO BE A MESSENGER AND WAS SENT TO GUIDE THE PEOPLE TOWARDS THE PATH OF RIGHTEOUSNESS AND FAITH.

PROPHET ISA HAD MANY MIRACLES AND TEACHINGS, AND HE PREACHED THE IMPORTANCE OF LOVE, COMPASSION, AND FORGIVENESS. HE ALSO PERFORMED MANY MIRACLES, SUCH AS HEALING THE SICK, RAISING THE DEAD, AND FEEDING THE HUNGRY.

PROPHET ISA'S MESSAGE WAS NOT ACCEPTED BY ALL, AND HE FACED MANY CHALLENGES AND OPPOSITION FROM THE PEOPLE IN POWER. HOWEVER, HE CONTINUED TO SPREAD HIS MESSAGE OF LOVE AND FAITH WITH GREAT PATIENCE AND PERSEVERANCE.

ONE OF THE MOST FAMOUS STORIES OF PROPHET ISA IS THE MIRACLE OF THE BIRDS. ONE DAY, PROPHET ISA WAS TRAVELING WITH HIS DISCIPLES WHEN THEY SAW A GROUP OF BIRDS LYING MOTIONLESS ON THE GROUND. PROPHET ISA APPROACHED THEM AND BREATHED ON THEM, AND THEY CAME BACK TO LIFE AND FLEW AWAY.

THIS MIRACLE WAS A POWERFUL
DEMONSTRATION OF THE POWER OF ALLAH
AND THE TRUTH OF PROPHET ISA'S MESSAGE.
IT SHOWED THAT ALLAH HAS POWER OVER ALL
THINGS, EVEN LIFE AND DEATH.

PROPHET ISA'S TEACHINGS AND MIRACLES
INSPIRED MANY PEOPLE, AND HIS MESSAGE OF
LOVE AND COMPASSION CONTINUES TO
INSPIRE PEOPLE TO THIS DAY. HE IS HIGHLY
RESPECTED IN ISLAM AS A PROPHET AND
MESSENGER OF ALLAH.

THE STORY OF PROPHET ISA TEACHES US THE
IMPORTANCE OF LOVE, COMPASSION, AND
FORGIVENESS, AND THE POWER OF FAITH AND
PATIENCE IN THE FACE OF ADVERSITY. IT ALSO
REMINDS US OF THE BLESSINGS OF ALLAH AND
THE IMPORTANCE OF FOLLOWING HIS
GUIDANCE.

AND WITH THAT, THE LITTLE ONE DRIFTED OFF
TO SLEEP, DREAMING OF THE TEACHINGS AND
MIRACLES OF PROPHET ISA AND THE GUIDANCE
AND BLESSINGS OF ALLAH.

THE STORY OF THE PROPHET YUNUS

ONCE UPON A TIME, THERE WAS A PROPHET
NAMED YUNUS (JONAH) WHO WAS SENT BY
ALLAH TO GUIDE THE PEOPLE OF NINEVEH.
HOWEVER, THE PEOPLE DID NOT LISTEN TO HIS
MESSAGE AND CONTINUED TO DISOBEY ALLAH'S
COMMANDMENTS.

FEELING DISCOURAGED, PROPHET YUNUS
DECIDED TO LEAVE NINEVEH AND TRAVELED BY
BOAT. HOWEVER, ALLAH SENT A GREAT STORM
TO THE SEA, AND THE BOAT WAS IN DANGER OF
SINKING. THE SAILORS REALIZED THAT THE
STORM WAS A PUNISHMENT FROM ALLAH AND
DECIDED TO CAST LOTS TO DETERMINE WHO
WAS RESPONSIBLE FOR THE DISASTER

THE LOT FELL ON PROPHET YUNUS, AND HE
REALIZED THAT HE HAD DISOBEYED ALLAH'S
COMMAND BY LEAVING NINEVEH WITHOUT
COMPLETING HIS MISSION. HE ASKED THE
SAILORS TO THROW HIM OVERBOARD AND WAS
SWALLOWED BY A LARGE FISH.

INSIDE THE FISH, PROPHET YUNUS REALIZED THE
ERROR OF HIS WAYS AND REPENTED TO ALLAH.
HE SPENT THREE DAYS AND NIGHTS IN THE
FISH'S BELLY, PRAYING AND SEEKING ALLAH'S
FORGIVENESS.

FINALLY, ALLAH HEARD HIS PRAYERS AND
COMMANDED THE FISH TO SPIT HIM OUT ON
THE SHORE. PROPHET YUNUS RETURNED TO
NINEVEH AND RESUMED HIS MISSION OF
CALLING THE PEOPLE TO ALLAH'S PATH

THIS TIME, THE PEOPLE LISTENED TO HIS
MESSAGE AND REPENTED TO ALLAH. THEY
CHANGED THEIR WAYS AND FOLLOWED
ALLAH'S COMMANDMENTS, AND ALLAH
FORGAVE THEM.

THE STORY OF PROPHET YUNUS TEACHES US
THE IMPORTANCE OF OBEDIENCE TO ALLAH'S
COMMANDMENTS, EVEN IN THE FACE OF
DIFFICULTIES AND CHALLENGES. IT ALSO
REMINDS US OF THE POWER OF REPENTANCE
AND THE MERCY OF ALLAH.

AND WITH THAT, THE LITTLE ONE DRIFTED OFF
TO SLEEP, DREAMING OF THE GUIDANCE AND
MERCY OF ALLAH AND THE TEACHINGS OF
PROPHET YUNUS.

THE STORY OF THE PROPHET HUD

ONCE UPON A TIME, THERE WAS A PROPHET
NAMED HUD WHO WAS SENT BY ALLAH TO
GUIDE THE PEOPLE OF 'AD. THE PEOPLE OF
'AD WERE KNOWN FOR THEIR STRENGTH
AND WEALTH, BUT THEY HAD BECOME
ARROGANT AND DISOBEDIENT TO ALLAH'S
COMMANDMENTS.

PROPHET HUD CALLED UPON THE PEOPLE
TO REPENT AND RETURN TO THE PATH OF
RIGHTEOUSNESS. HE REMINDED THEM OF
THE BLESSINGS OF ALLAH AND WARNED
THEM OF THE CONSEQUENCES OF THEIR
DISOBEDIENCE.

HOWEVER, THE PEOPLE OF 'AD REFUSED TO
LISTEN TO HIS MESSAGE AND MOCKED HIM.
THEY CHALLENGED HIM TO BRING UPON
THEM THE PUNISHMENT HE WAS WARNING
THEM ABOUT.

IN RESPONSE, ALLAH SENT A POWERFUL WIND
THAT LASTED FOR SEVEN NIGHTS AND EIGHT
DAYS, DESTROYING EVERYTHING IN ITS PATH

THE PEOPLE OF 'AD WERE UNABLE TO
WITHSTAND THE FORCE OF THE WIND AND
WERE DESTROYED, EXCEPT FOR THOSE WHO
BELIEVED IN ALLAH AND FOLLOWED THE
GUIDANCE OF PROPHET HUD.

THE STORY OF PROPHET HUD TEACHES US
THE IMPORTANCE OF OBEDIENCE TO ALLAH'S
COMMANDMENTS AND THE CONSEQUENCES
OF DISOBEDIENCE. IT ALSO REMINDS US OF
THE BLESSINGS OF ALLAH AND THE
IMPORTANCE OF GRATITUDE FOR HIS FAVORS

AND WITH THAT, THE LITTLE ONE DRIFTED OFF
TO SLEEP, DREAMING OF THE GUIDANCE AND
MERCY OF ALLAH AND THE TEACHINGS OF
PROPHET HUD.

THE STORY OF
THE PROPHET IBRAHIM'S SACRIFICE

ONCE UPON A TIME, THERE WAS A PROPHET NAMED IBRAHIM (ABRAHAM) WHO LOVED ALLAH WITH ALL HIS HEART. ALLAH HAD BLESSED HIM WITH A SON NAMED ISMAIL (ISHMAEL), AND IBRAHIM LOVED HIM DEARLY.

ONE NIGHT, IBRAHIM HAD A DREAM IN WHICH ALLAH COMMANDED HIM TO SACRIFICE HIS SON AS A TEST OF HIS FAITH. IBRAHIM WAS HEARTBROKEN BUT KNEW THAT HE HAD TO OBEY ALLAH'S COMMAND.

THE NEXT MORNING, IBRAHIM TOLD HIS SON ISMAIL ABOUT THE DREAM AND THE COMMANDMENT HE HAD RECEIVED FROM ALLAH. ISMAIL WAS ALSO A RIGHTEOUS AND OBEDIENT SON, AND HE IMMEDIATELY AGREED TO FULFILL ALLAH'S COMMAND.

TOGETHER, IBRAHIM AND ISMAIL SET OUT TO THE PLACE OF SACRIFICE. ALONG THE WAY, SATAN TRIED TO TEMPT IBRAHIM TO DISOBEY ALLAH, BUT IBRAHIM RESISTED AND THREW STONES AT SATAN TO DRIVE HIM AWAY.

WHEN THEY ARRIVED AT THE PLACE OF
SACRIFICE, IBRAHIM PREPARED TO SACRIFICE HIS
BELOVED SON ISMAIL. BUT JUST AS HE WAS
ABOUT TO DO SO, ALLAH SENT A RAM TO
REPLACE ISMAIL, AS A SIGN OF IBRAHIM'S
UNWAVERING FAITH AND OBEDIENCE.

ALLAH WAS PLEASED WITH IBRAHIM'S DEVOTION
AND SACRIFICE, AND HE DECLARED THAT
IBRAHIM'S EXAMPLE WOULD BE REMEMBERED
FOR GENERATIONS TO COME

THE STORY OF IBRAHIM'S SACRIFICE TEACHES
US THE IMPORTANCE OF OBEDIENCE TO
ALLAH'S COMMANDMENTS, EVEN WHEN IT IS
DIFFICULT OR GOES AGAINST OUR DESIRES. IT
ALSO REMINDS US OF THE BLESSINGS OF
ALLAH AND THE IMPORTANCE OF GRATITUDE
FOR HIS FAVORS.

AND WITH THAT, THE LITTLE ONE DRIFTED OFF
TO SLEEP, DREAMING OF THE GUIDANCE AND
MERCY OF ALLAH AND THE EXAMPLE OF
PROPHET IBRAHIM'S SACRIFICE.

THE STORY OF THE PROPHET SHUAIB

ONCE UPON A TIME, THERE WAS A PROPHET NAMED SHUAIB WHO WAS SENT BY ALLAH TO GUIDE THE PEOPLE OF MADYAN. THE PEOPLE OF MADYAN WERE KNOWN FOR THEIR DISHONESTY AND MISTREATMENT OF OTHERS, AND THEY HAD STRAYED FROM THE PATH OF RIGHTEOUSNESS.

PROPHET SHUAIB CALLED UPON THE PEOPLE TO REPENT AND RETURN TO THE PATH OF ALLAH. HE REMINDED THEM OF THE IMPORTANCE OF JUSTICE AND FAIRNESS AND WARNED THEM OF THE CONSEQUENCES OF THEIR ACTIONS.

HOWEVER, THE PEOPLE OF MADYAN REFUSED TO LISTEN TO HIS MESSAGE AND CONTINUED TO MISTREAT OTHERS AND ENGAGE IN DISHONEST PRACTICES. THEY EVEN THREATENED PROPHET SHUAIB AND HIS FOLLOWERS, BUT HE REMAINED STEADFAST IN HIS MISSION.

IN RESPONSE, ALLAH SENT A POWERFUL EARTHQUAKE THAT DESTROYED THE HOMES AND LANDS OF THE PEOPLE OF MADYAN. THE BELIEVERS WERE SAVED, BUT THE NON-BELIEVERS WERE PUNISHED FOR THEIR WRONGDOING.

THE STORY OF PROPHET SHUAIB TEACHES US THE IMPORTANCE OF JUSTICE AND FAIRNESS IN OUR DEALINGS WITH OTHERS. IT ALSO REMINDS US OF THE CONSEQUENCES OF OUR ACTIONS AND THE IMPORTANCE OF REPENTANCE AND SEEKING ALLAH'S FORGIVENESS.

AND WITH THAT, THE LITTLE ONE DRIFTED OFF TO SLEEP, DREAMING OF THE GUIDANCE AND MERCY OF ALLAH AND THE TEACHINGS OF PROPHET SHUAIB.

THE STORY OF THE PROPHET NUH

ONCE UPON A TIME, THERE WAS A PROPHET NAMED NUH (NOAH) WHO WAS SENT BY ALLAH TO GUIDE THE PEOPLE OF HIS TIME. THE PEOPLE HAD BECOME ARROGANT AND DISOBEDIENT TO ALLAH'S COMMANDMENTS, AND NUH WAS TASKED WITH WARNING THEM OF THE CONSEQUENCES OF THEIR ACTIONS.

PROPHET NUH CALLED UPON THE PEOPLE TO REPENT AND RETURN TO THE PATH OF RIGHTEOUSNESS. HE REMINDED THEM OF THE BLESSINGS OF ALLAH AND WARNED THEM OF THE PUNISHMENT THAT AWAITED THEM IF THEY CONTINUED ON THEIR SINFUL PATH.

HOWEVER, THE PEOPLE OF NUH REFUSED TO LISTEN TO HIS MESSAGE AND MOCKED HIM. THEY CHALLENGED HIM TO BRING UPON THEM THE PUNISHMENT HE WAS WARNING THEM ABOUT.

IN RESPONSE, ALLAH COMMANDED NUH TO BUILD A GREAT ARK, AND HE INSTRUCTED NUH TO TAKE ABOARD THE ARK HIS FAMILY, A PAIR OF EVERY KIND OF ANIMAL, AND THOSE WHO BELIEVED IN ALLAH AND FOLLOWED THE GUIDANCE OF PROPHET NUH.

AS THE FLOODWATERS ROSE AND
DESTROYED EVERYTHING IN THEIR PATH,
THE ARK FLOATED SAFELY ABOVE THE
WATER, CARRYING THOSE WHO BELIEVED
AND HAD REPENTED.

AFTER THE FLOODWATERS RECEDED AND
THE ARK CAME TO REST ON A
MOUNTAINTOP, ALLAH MADE A COVENANT
WITH NUH THAT HE WOULD NEVER AGAIN
DESTROY THE EARTH WITH A FLOOD.

THE STORY OF PROPHET NUH TEACHES US
THE IMPORTANCE OF OBEDIENCE TO
ALLAH'S COMMANDMENTS AND THE
CONSEQUENCES OF DISOBEDIENCE. IT ALSO
REMINDS US OF THE BLESSINGS OF ALLAH
AND THE IMPORTANCE OF GRATITUDE FOR
HIS FAVORS.

AND WITH THAT, THE LITTLE ONE DRIFTED
OFF TO SLEEP, DREAMING OF THE
GUIDANCE AND MERCY OF ALLAH AND THE
TEACHINGS OF PROPHET NUH.

THE STORY OF THE PROPHET SALEH

ONCE UPON A TIME, THERE WAS A PROPHET NAMED SALEH WHO WAS SENT BY ALLAH TO GUIDE THE PEOPLE OF THAMUD. THE PEOPLE OF THAMUD HAD BECOME ARROGANT AND HAD STARTED WORSHIPPING IDOLS, INSTEAD OF FOLLOWING THE GUIDANCE OF ALLAH.

PROPHET SALEH CALLED UPON THE PEOPLE TO REPENT AND RETURN TO THE PATH OF RIGHTEOUSNESS. HE REMINDED THEM OF THE BLESSINGS OF ALLAH AND WARNED THEM OF THE PUNISHMENT THAT AWAITED THEM IF THEY CONTINUED ON THEIR SINFUL PATH.

HOWEVER, THE PEOPLE OF THAMUD REFUSED TO LISTEN TO HIS MESSAGE AND MOCKED HIM. THEY CHALLENGED HIM TO SHOW THEM A SIGN OF ALLAH'S POWER AND MIGHT.

IN RESPONSE, ALLAH GRANTED PROPHET SALEH THE ABILITY TO PERFORM A MIRACLE. HE SHOWED THEM A PREGNANT SHE-CAMEL THAT WAS A GIFT FROM ALLAH AND INSTRUCTED THE PEOPLE TO TAKE CARE OF HER AND TREAT HER KINDLY.

BUT THE PEOPLE OF THAMUD DID NOT HEED
THE INSTRUCTIONS OF PROPHET SALEH. THEY
ABUSED THE SHE-CAMEL AND KILLED HER,
IGNORING THE WARNINGS OF ALLAH.

AS A PUNISHMENT, ALLAH SENT A POWERFUL
EARTHQUAKE THAT DESTROYED THE HOMES
AND LANDS OF THE PEOPLE OF THAMUD. THE
BELIEVERS WERE SAVED, BUT THE NON-
BELIEVERS WERE PUNISHED FOR THEIR
WRONGDOING.

THE STORY OF PROPHET SALEH TEACHES US
THE IMPORTANCE OF OBEDIENCE TO ALLAH'S
COMMANDMENTS AND THE CONSEQUENCES
OF DISOBEDIENCE. IT ALSO REMINDS US OF
THE BLESSINGS OF ALLAH AND THE
IMPORTANCE OF TREATING ALL OF ALLAH'S
CREATIONS WITH KINDNESS AND COMPASSION.

AND WITH THAT, THE LITTLE ONE DRIFTED OFF
TO SLEEP, DREAMING OF THE GUIDANCE AND
MERCY OF ALLAH AND THE TEACHINGS OF
PROPHET SALEH.

THE STORY OF THE PROPHET LUT

ONCE UPON A TIME, THERE WAS A PROPHET NAMED LUT WHO WAS SENT BY ALLAH TO GUIDE THE PEOPLE OF SODOM AND GOMORRAH. THE PEOPLE OF THESE CITIES HAD BECOME ARROGANT AND DISOBEDIENT TO ALLAH'S COMMANDMENTS, AND LUT WAS TASKED WITH WARNING THEM OF THE CONSEQUENCES OF THEIR ACTIONS.

PROPHET LUT CALLED UPON THE PEOPLE TO REPENT AND RETURN TO THE PATH OF RIGHTEOUSNESS. HE REMINDED THEM OF THE BLESSINGS OF ALLAH AND WARNED THEM OF THE PUNISHMENT THAT AWAITED THEM IF THEY CONTINUED ON THEIR SINFUL PATH.

HOWEVER, THE PEOPLE OF SODOM AND GOMORRAH REFUSED TO LISTEN TO HIS MESSAGE AND MOCKED HIM. THEY CHALLENGED HIM TO BRING UPON THEM THE PUNISHMENT HE WAS WARNING THEM ABOUT.

IN RESPONSE, ALLAH SENT TWO ANGELS IN THE FORM OF HANDSOME YOUNG MEN TO TEST THE PEOPLE OF SODOM AND GOMORRAH. THE ANGELS WERE WELCOMED BY PROPHET LUT AND HIS FAMILY, BUT THE PEOPLE OF THE CITIES WANTED TO HARM THEM.

48

THE ANGELS WARNED PROPHET LUT TO
LEAVE THE CITIES BEFORE THE PUNISHMENT
OF ALLAH WAS UNLEASHED UPON THEM.
PROPHET LUT AND HIS FAMILY FLED THE
CITIES, AND ALLAH SENT DOWN A RAIN OF
STONES UPON THE PEOPLE OF SODOM
AND GOMORRAH, DESTROYING THEM AND
THEIR LANDS.

THE STORY OF PROPHET LUT TEACHES US
THE IMPORTANCE OF OBEDIENCE TO
ALLAH'S COMMANDMENTS AND THE
CONSEQUENCES OF DISOBEDIENCE. IT ALSO
REMINDS US OF THE BLESSINGS OF ALLAH
AND THE IMPORTANCE OF SHOWING
KINDNESS AND HOSPITALITY TO GUESTS,
EVEN IF THEY ARE STRANGERS.

AND WITH THAT, THE LITTLE ONE DRIFTED
OFF TO SLEEP, DREAMING OF THE
GUIDANCE AND MERCY OF ALLAH AND THE
TEACHINGS OF PROPHET LUT.

THE STORY OF THE PROPHET AYYUB

ONCE UPON A TIME, THERE WAS A PROPHET NAMED AYYUB (JOB) WHO WAS BLESSED BY ALLAH WITH GREAT WEALTH, A HAPPY FAMILY, AND GOOD HEALTH. HOWEVER, ONE DAY, ALLAH TESTED PROPHET AYYUB BY TAKING AWAY HIS WEALTH, HIS FAMILY, AND HIS HEALTH.

DESPITE HIS HARDSHIPS, PROPHET AYYUB NEVER LOST FAITH IN ALLAH AND REMAINED PATIENT AND GRATEFUL. HE CONTINUED TO PRAY AND SEEK ALLAH'S MERCY, EVEN WHEN HE WAS AFFLICTED WITH A PAINFUL SKIN DISEASE THAT MADE HIM AN OUTCAST IN HIS COMMUNITY.

PROPHET AYYUB'S WIFE AND FRIENDS ADVISED HIM TO CURSE ALLAH AND GIVE UP ON HIS FAITH, BUT HE REFUSED TO DO SO. HE TRUSTED IN ALLAH'S WISDOM AND KNEW THAT HIS SUFFERING WAS A TEST OF HIS FAITH AND DEVOTION.

FINALLY, AFTER MANY YEARS OF PATIENCE
AND PRAYER, ALLAH HEARD PROPHET AYYUB'S
PRAYERS AND RESTORED HIS HEALTH, HIS
FAMILY, AND HIS WEALTH. PROPHET AYYUB
THANKED ALLAH FOR HIS MERCY AND
BLESSINGS, AND HIS STORY BECAME A
POWERFUL EXAMPLE OF FAITH AND
PERSEVERANCE

THE STORY OF PROPHET AYYUB TEACHES US
THE IMPORTANCE OF PATIENCE, GRATITUDE,
AND FAITH IN ALLAH, EVEN DURING TIMES OF
HARDSHIP AND ADVERSITY. IT ALSO REMINDS
US OF THE POWER OF PRAYER AND THE
IMPORTANCE OF SEEKING ALLAH'S MERCY
AND GUIDANCE IN ALL ASPECTS OF OUR LIVES.

AND WITH THAT, THE LITTLE ONE DRIFTED
OFF TO SLEEP, DREAMING OF THE GUIDANCE
AND MERCY OF ALLAH AND THE TEACHINGS
OF PROPHET AYYUB.

THE STORY OF THE PROPHET YAQUB

ONCE UPON A TIME, THERE WAS A PROPHET NAMED YAQUB (JACOB) WHO WAS BLESSED WITH MANY CHILDREN. HOWEVER, YAQUB LOVED ONE OF HIS SONS, YUSUF (JOSEPH), MORE THAN THE OTHERS, WHICH MADE HIS OTHER SONS JEALOUS AND RESENTFUL.

ONE DAY, YUSUF'S BROTHERS DECIDED TO GET RID OF HIM BY THROWING HIM INTO A WELL AND TELLING THEIR FATHER THAT HE HAD BEEN KILLED BY A WILD ANIMAL. YAQUB WAS HEARTBROKEN AND MOURNED THE LOSS OF HIS BELOVED SON FOR MANY YEARS.

MEANWHILE, YUSUF WAS FOUND BY A GROUP OF TRAVELERS WHO SOLD HIM AS A SLAVE IN EGYPT. DESPITE HIS HARDSHIPS, YUSUF REMAINED FAITHFUL TO ALLAH AND ROSE TO BECOME A TRUSTED ADVISOR TO THE PHARAOH OF EGYPT.

YEARS LATER, DURING A FAMINE, YAQUB
AND HIS SONS TRAVELED TO EGYPT IN
SEARCH OF FOOD. THERE, THEY WERE
REUNITED WITH YUSUF, WHO HAD
BECOME A POWERFUL AND INFLUENTIAL
FIGURE IN THE LAND.

YUSUF FORGAVE HIS BROTHERS FOR
THEIR ACTIONS AND WELCOMED HIS
FAMILY TO EGYPT. YAQUB WAS
OVERJOYED TO BE REUNITED WITH HIS
SON AND HIS FAITH IN ALLAH WAS
RENEWED.

THE STORY OF PROPHET YAQUB
TEACHES US THE IMPORTANCE OF LOVE,
FORGIVENESS, AND TRUST IN ALLAH'S
PLAN. IT ALSO REMINDS US THAT EVEN IN
TIMES OF HARDSHIP AND ADVERSITY, WE
MUST REMAIN FAITHFUL AND TRUST IN
ALLAH'S GUIDANCE.

AND WITH THAT, THE LITTLE ONE DRIFTED
OFF TO SLEEP, DREAMING OF THE
GUIDANCE AND MERCY OF ALLAH AND
THE TEACHINGS OF PROPHET YAQUB.

THE STORY
OF THE PROPHET IBRAHIM AND THE FIRE

ONCE UPON A TIME, THERE WAS A PROPHET
NAMED IBRAHIM (ABRAHAM) WHO WAS
DEVOTED TO ALLAH AND SPREAD THE
MESSAGE OF ISLAM TO HIS PEOPLE.
HOWEVER, THE PEOPLE OF IBRAHIM'S
COMMUNITY DID NOT BELIEVE IN ALLAH AND
WERE HOSTILE TOWARDS HIS TEACHINGS.

ONE DAY, THE PEOPLE OF IBRAHIM'S
COMMUNITY DECIDED TO PUNISH HIM FOR HIS
BELIEFS BY THROWING HIM INTO A HUGE FIRE.
AS THEY LIT THE FIRE, IBRAHIM CALLED OUT
TO ALLAH, SEEKING HIS HELP AND
PROTECTION.

TO EVERYONE'S AMAZEMENT, ALLAH
ANSWERED IBRAHIM'S PRAYERS BY
COMMANDING THE FIRE TO BECOME COOL
AND PEACEFUL. AS A RESULT, IBRAHIM WAS
ABLE TO WALK OUT OF THE FIRE UNHARMED,
AND THE PEOPLE OF HIS COMMUNITY WERE
LEFT IN AWE OF ALLAH'S POWER AND MERCY.

THE STORY OF PROPHET IBRAHIM AND THE FIRE TEACHES US THE IMPORTANCE OF FAITH AND TRUST IN ALLAH. IT REMINDS US THAT EVEN IN THE FACE OF ADVERSITY AND DANGER, ALLAH HAS THE POWER TO PROTECT US AND GUIDE US TOWARDS THE RIGHT PATH.

AND WITH THAT, THE LITTLE ONE DRIFTED OFF TO SLEEP, DREAMING OF THE GUIDANCE AND MERCY OF ALLAH AND THE TEACHINGS OF PROPHET IBRAHIM.

THE STORY OF
THE PROPHET ISA AND THE MIRACLE
OF THE BIRDS

ONCE UPON A TIME, THERE WAS A PROPHET
NAMED ISA (JESUS) WHO WAS LOVED AND
RESPECTED BY HIS FOLLOWERS FOR HIS KIND
AND COMPASSIONATE NATURE. ONE DAY, AS ISA
WAS WALKING THROUGH A FIELD WITH HIS
DISCIPLES, A GROUP OF BIRDS FLEW DOWN AND
BEGAN TO CHIRP AND SING AROUND HIM.

ISA'S DISCIPLES WERE AMAZED AND ASKED HOW
HE WAS ABLE TO COMMUNICATE WITH THE
BIRDS. ISA REPLIED THAT IT WAS A MIRACLE
FROM ALLAH AND THAT ALLAH HAD GIVEN HIM
THE ABILITY TO UNDERSTAND AND SPEAK THE
LANGUAGE OF ALL CREATURES.

TO DEMONSTRATE THIS, ISA REACHED OUT
HIS HAND AND CALLED THE BIRDS TO COME
AND LAND ON IT. TO EVERYONE'S
AMAZEMENT, THE BIRDS FLEW DOWN AND
PERCHED ON HIS HAND AND SHOULDER,
SINGING AND CHIRPING JOYFULLY.

THE STORY OF PROPHET ISA AND THE
MIRACLE OF THE BIRDS TEACHES US THE
IMPORTANCE OF COMPASSION AND RESPECT
FOR ALL CREATURES. IT REMINDS US THAT
ALLAH HAS GIVEN US THE RESPONSIBILITY TO
CARE FOR AND PROTECT THE NATURAL
WORLD, AND THAT WE SHOULD TREAT ALL
LIVING BEINGS WITH KINDNESS AND
COMPASSION.

AND WITH THAT, THE LITTLE ONE DRIFTED
OFF TO SLEEP, DREAMING OF THE GUIDANCE
AND MERCY OF ALLAH AND THE TEACHINGS
OF PROPHET ISA.

THE STORY OF PROPHET YUNUS AND THE PEOPLE OF NINEVEH

ONCE UPON A TIME, THERE WAS A PROPHET NAMED YUNUS (JONAH) WHO WAS SENT BY ALLAH TO PREACH TO THE PEOPLE OF NINEVEH, A CITY KNOWN FOR ITS WICKEDNESS AND CORRUPTION. HOWEVER, THE PEOPLE OF NINEVEH DID NOT LISTEN TO YUNUS AND CONTINUED TO LIVE IN SIN AND DISOBEDIENCE.

FEELING FRUSTRATED AND HOPELESS, YUNUS LEFT THE CITY AND BOARDED A SHIP TO ESCAPE FROM THE PEOPLE OF NINEVEH. HOWEVER, AS THE SHIP SAILED ON, A FIERCE STORM AROSE AND THREATENED TO SINK THE SHIP. THE CREW REALIZED THAT SOMEONE ON THE SHIP MUST HAVE ANGERED THEIR GODS AND DECIDED TO CAST LOTS TO DETERMINE WHO WAS TO BLAME. THE LOT FELL ON YUNUS, AND HE WAS THROWN OVERBOARD INTO THE SEA.

AS HE SANK DEEPER INTO THE WATER, YUNUS CALLED OUT TO ALLAH FOR HELP AND FORGIVENESS. ALLAH ANSWERED HIS PRAYERS BY SENDING A GIANT FISH TO SWALLOW YUNUS AND PROTECT HIM FROM DROWNING. YUNUS SPENT THREE DAYS AND THREE NIGHTS INSIDE THE BELLY OF THE FISH, PRAYING AND SEEKING ALLAH'S FORGIVENESS.

FINALLY, ALLAH COMMANDED THE FISH TO RELEASE YUNUS, AND HE WAS WASHED UP ON THE SHORE. REALIZING THE ERROR OF HIS WAYS, YUNUS RETURNED TO THE PEOPLE OF NINEVEH AND PREACHED TO THEM AGAIN. THIS TIME, THE PEOPLE LISTENED AND REPENTED THEIR SINS, AND ALLAH SHOWED THEM MERCY AND FORGIVENESS.

THE STORY OF PROPHET YUNUS AND THE PEOPLE OF NINEVEH TEACHES US THE IMPORTANCE OF REPENTANCE AND SEEKING FORGIVENESS FROM ALLAH. IT REMINDS US THAT ALLAH IS MERCIFUL AND FORGIVING, AND THAT WE SHOULD ALWAYS STRIVE TO DO WHAT IS RIGHT AND FOLLOW THE PATH OF RIGHTEOUSNESS.

AND WITH THAT, THE LITTLE ONE DRIFTED OFF TO SLEEP, DREAMING OF THE GUIDANCE AND MERCY OF ALLAH AND THE TEACHINGS OF PROPHET YUNUS.

THE STORY OF THE COMPANIONS OF THE PROPHET MUHAMMAD

ONCE UPON A TIME, THERE LIVED A PROPHET NAMED MUHAMMAD (PEACE BE UPON HIM) WHO WAS SENT BY ALLAH TO GUIDE HUMANITY TOWARDS THE PATH OF RIGHTEOUSNESS. THE PROPHET MUHAMMAD HAD MANY COMPANIONS WHO LOVED AND RESPECTED HIM FOR HIS WISDOM AND GUIDANCE.

THE COMPANIONS OF THE PROPHET MUHAMMAD WERE MEN AND WOMEN WHO BELIEVED IN ALLAH AND THE MESSAGE OF THE PROPHET. THEY DEVOTED THEIR LIVES TO SPREADING THE MESSAGE OF ISLAM AND LIVING A LIFE OF COMPASSION, KINDNESS, AND JUSTICE.

THE COMPANIONS OF THE PROPHET MUHAMMAD WERE ALSO KNOWN FOR THEIR BRAVERY AND COURAGE. THEY STOOD BY THE PROPHET IN TIMES OF HARDSHIP AND FACED PERSECUTION AND HARDSHIP FOR THE SAKE OF ALLAH. THEY WERE KNOWN FOR THEIR SELFLESSNESS AND GENEROSITY, ALWAYS PUTTING THE NEEDS OF OTHERS BEFORE THEIR OWN.

ONE OF THE MOST FAMOUS COMPANIONS
OF THE PROPHET MUHAMMAD WAS ABU
BAKR, WHO WAS THE PROPHET'S
CLOSEST FRIEND AND ADVISOR. ANOTHER
COMPANION WAS UMAR, WHO LATER
BECAME THE SECOND CALIPH OF ISLAM.
OTHER NOTABLE COMPANIONS INCLUDE
ALI, FATIMA, AND AISHA, WHO WERE ALL
RELATED TO THE PROPHET MUHAMMAD

THE STORIES OF THE COMPANIONS OF
THE PROPHET MUHAMMAD TEACH US THE
IMPORTANCE OF DEVOTION TO ALLAH AND
THE PROPHET. THEY REMIND US OF THE
SACRIFICES AND HARDSHIPS THAT WERE
FACED BY THE EARLY MUSLIMS, AND THE
IMPORTANCE OF FOLLOWING THE PATH
OF RIGHTEOUSNESS.

AND WITH THAT, THE LITTLE ONE DRIFTED
OFF TO SLEEP, DREAMING OF THE
GUIDANCE AND MERCY OF ALLAH AND THE
NOBLE COMPANIONS OF THE PROPHET
MUHAMMAD.

THE STORY OF THE LAST PROPHET

ONCE UPON A TIME, IN THE CITY OF MECCA, THERE WAS A MAN NAMED MUHAMMAD WHO WAS BORN INTO THE TRIBE OF QURAYSH. HE WAS KNOWN FOR HIS HONESTY, KINDNESS, AND WISDOM. AS A YOUNG MAN, HE WOULD OFTEN SPEND TIME ALONE IN THE MOUNTAINS, MEDITATING AND REFLECTING ON LIFE.

ONE DAY, WHILE MEDITATING IN A CAVE ON THE OUTSKIRTS OF MECCA, THE ANGEL GABRIEL APPEARED TO MUHAMMAD AND REVEALED TO HIM THAT HE WAS CHOSEN BY ALLAH TO BE HIS LAST PROPHET AND MESSENGER TO HUMANITY. THE REVELATION CAME IN THE FORM OF THE FIRST VERSES OF THE QURAN, WHICH WERE RECITED TO HIM BY GABRIEL.

MUHAMMAD WAS INITIALLY FRIGHTENED BY THE EXPERIENCE, BUT HIS WIFE KHADIJAH COMFORTED HIM AND ENCOURAGED HIM TO EMBRACE HIS ROLE AS A PROPHET. HE BEGAN PREACHING THE MESSAGE OF ISLAM, WHICH CALLED FOR THE WORSHIP OF ALLAH AND THE PURSUIT OF RIGHTEOUSNESS AND JUSTICE

THE PEOPLE OF MECCA WERE INITIALLY SKEPTICAL OF MUHAMMAD'S MESSAGE, BUT SOME BEGAN TO CONVERT AFTER WITNESSING HIS CHARACTER AND SINCERITY. HOWEVER, THE POWERFUL LEADERS OF MECCA FELT THREATENED BY HIS TEACHINGS, WHICH CHALLENGED THEIR AUTHORITY AND WAY OF LIFE.

62

THE PROPHET MUHAMMAD FACED PERSECUTION
AND HARDSHIP FOR MANY YEARS, BUT HE
REMAINED STEADFAST IN HIS MISSION TO
SPREAD THE MESSAGE OF ISLAM. HE MIGRATED
TO MEDINA WITH HIS FOLLOWERS, WHERE HE
ESTABLISHED THE FIRST ISLAMIC COMMUNITY.

THROUGH HIS TEACHINGS AND EXAMPLE, THE
PROPHET MUHAMMAD TRANSFORMED ARABIA
AND THE WORLD. HE EMPHASIZED THE
IMPORTANCE OF COMPASSION, KINDNESS, AND
JUSTICE, AND HE INSPIRED HIS FOLLOWERS TO
LIVE ACCORDING TO THESE PRINCIPLES.

TODAY, OVER 1 BILLION PEOPLE AROUND THE
WORLD FOLLOW THE TEACHINGS OF THE
PROPHET MUHAMMAD AND HIS MESSAGE OF
ISLAM. HIS LEGACY CONTINUES TO INSPIRE
PEOPLE OF ALL AGES AND BACKGROUNDS TO
STRIVE FOR GOODNESS, RIGHTEOUSNESS, AND
PEACE.

AND WITH THAT, THE LITTLE ONE DRIFTED OFF
TO SLEEP, DREAMING OF THE LAST PROPHET
AND HIS MESSAGE OF LOVE AND COMPASSION.

DEAR MUSLIM PARENTS,

I WOULD LIKE TO EXPRESS MY SINCERE GRATITUDE FOR CHOOSING MY RAMADAN BEDTIME STORIES BOOK FOR YOUR KIDS. I HOPE THAT THE STORIES HAVE BEEN BOTH ENTERTAINING AND EDUCATIONAL FOR THEM, HELPING THEM TO LEARN MORE ABOUT ISLAM AND THE IMPORTANCE OF RAMADAN.

YOUR SUPPORT AND TRUST MEAN THE WORLD TO ME, AND I AM HONORED TO HAVE BEEN A PART OF YOUR FAMILY'S RAMADAN TRADITIONS. IT IS MY HOPE THAT THE STORIES HAVE HELPED TO CREATE LASTING MEMORIES FOR YOUR CHILDREN.

IF YOU HAVE A MOMENT, I WOULD KINDLY ASK FOR YOUR FEEDBACK BY LEAVING A REVIEW ON AMAZON. YOUR REVIEW WILL HELP OTHER PARENTS MAKE INFORMED DECISIONS WHEN CONSIDERING PURCHASING THE BOOK, AND IT WILL ALSO HELP ME IMPROVE THE BOOK FOR FUTURE EDITIONS.

THANK YOU ONCE AGAIN FOR YOUR SUPPORT, AND I WISH YOU AND YOUR FAMILY A BLESSED RAMADAN.

BEST REGARDS,

AISHA

Made in the USA
Columbia, SC
02 March 2025

54574858R00037